Monica McClure

The Gone Thing

Winter Editions, 2023

PASTORAL I

We long for what
We had not

A serene progression of thoughts
Intimacy with streams and clouds
At home inside the wool of cloak

Once we did not graze on each other
Spiritually against everything

Time was something you were born with, or not

In our songs, we found a dry spell
Our staffs were like harvested polls

And we moved inside a system that suffered
But never died

The undeniable necessity of land
Makes me chew through life

Living makes me spit it out

INHERITANCE

I gave my youngest sister a spoonful of oats
I gave my younger sister the chance to be good

  I must lift the toilet seat to spray the grime
  and wipe and dig the swipe around the shit
  of the objects in the bathroom of the gas station
  and pull my ponytail through my red cap
  and accept the compliment, "You're not as
  lazy as she said you was," and hand the hot chicken
  to the woman who is three days sleepless with rage
  and offer to let her beat my ass
  with hands transformed into Swarovski crystals
  and eyes the color of uncooked meth

I gave my younger sister a marigold
I gave my youngest sister AI-generated perfume
I am the eldest sister and therefore a thief

  I must go back to the Southside Clubhouse
  The city pool where the water is acrid and mine
  to watch from the stand the bodies browner
  than my own and tamed by the Lion's Club
  It takes less than a whistle to summon cops
  Crawling up the walk reptilian sons of white hens
  Just to chat and glare standing under my thighs
  placing one pink hand near my foot the gold
  below the knuckle just sinews and chicken bone

I am the eldest sister and therefore wealthy

  I have to man the register the mother has left
  to nurse her sick child and at day's end
  I must find it short and alert the woman

without papers who got this job her first at 12
By saying 16 and an American citizen and though
She claims it's my mistake I hear it in the mother's
voice when I call But I also hear it when this woman
cries "They'll fire me," and I see her beads of pleas
that circle of prayers on her throat when she sobs
I'd played it before this big bow we do when risks fail
I could take this one I could afford to lose a job I'm 16
I've been known to make math mistakes to be high
and even to steal but we are all so innocent as clean
as the next broke girl with her plush bed of cons Her
lies The hairs she broke with a dollar store comb
are more split than leaves in a forest fire

I gave my younger sister a decent name
I gave my youngest sister bad advice

    I have to unfurl the hose and drag it from kennel
    to kennel spraying the shit into the drain
    under the watchful sun of community service
    It runs in brown rivulets and the stench is
    sad sick of spirit and terrified sweet more
    like an outpouring of defeat unlike the shit
    of humans which is recalcitrant and brash
    This summer I am not eating I am doing penance
    for a petty crime Nor am I buying the tail of this
    war a man speaks of as he twirls a possum
    like a lasso over his head, "They don't scare me,"
    he says He tread a river of dead bodies in Vietnam

My geraniums have been decapitated
by a creature with strong flat teeth

Father flinches at amputated limbs
His sober held still and high these days

I gave my youngest sister a Bishop's hat
I gave my younger sister a creeping blue star
It surrounded her son
like a cape of moss like the coat of Joseph
like a gasping magic breath
that made him appear golden and precious among the rot

   I am the eldest sister and therefore I must sort
   one paper from the next peering over an edge
   Where a blonde woman on her last leg has built a palace of
   beige dust in plain view of her employer Her fragile
   grip on the hem of her red skirt as she tugs knit over
   an unmoving chain of joints which she dragged to a corner
   of an attorney's office once and never returned From
   here I can watch women behind a bulletproof lens and
   tomorrow I'll put my body between a hedge fund and
   an elevator as the earth quakes her way up 32 floors
   How quaint these working girls in pencil skirts around the
   fountain unwrapping their lunches in 2012 calling
   their moms their roommates twirling their drizzle of day pearls
   turning magnificent tricks with every coffee stirrer
   pinched between chrome nails Their weight loss journals
   their savings their hangovers and schemes the husbands
   with second families on an island our sugar daddies
   our cocaine straws I'm wearing the dress she wore to
   her mother's funeral It's black and white I keep it and
   That night we dine on her dad's credit card I remember
   our need to be filled up The sound of her being penetrated
   as the tranquilizers wrapped me in a mother

Remember I don't have a mother I have another sister
I gave her a handbag on fire which she buries in the day
and exhumes at night like a firefly Coco Chanel of the frack lands

I gave my sisters rising flurries of pebbles which sumptuously
overflow their champagne flutes

I must speak to the boss over an empty desk as he
tilts in his pool of vodka and urine A buoy near an offshore
rig What can a man who has never worked teach me of
this work? So much, it seems He moves his father's
fortune from one property to the next peninsula A building
a sale a rental an asset a liquid tide coming in with
promises and contracts leveraged against my liable farm
beset with Bo weevil And when I move my hand to my mouth
to show him how we're living he says, "Go watch her. She's
not like us." So I walk to my seat and study the smooth wrist
of my friend at work every eyelash every greeting The gangster
realtor says somethings-in-it-for-me for us but what
A porky man reaches as if to strangle her neck
I pull at his haunches My friend and I scream No one
comes We don't call the cops We call the cops and later
when the hired guard is escorting us out
she demands, "Treat me as you would treat your own daughter."

Good news: hunger has ended in the United States!
It ended more than 50 years ago

I gave my younger sister an $18 cocktail
I gave my youngest sister microgreens dressed in preserved lemon
Ring pop yacht yacht yacht gunshot automatic
Yes I am talking about being poor in America
Suck my dick I am no longer poor I'm high-salaried

I lubricate the hinges of information design
with spit from my glands I write billions to you
Please attend would you in a cloud Every question you
put to it is gas vacuumed into cotton where it remains
Just put it up there put it right there put it where you need it
so you may always look up and feel paid floating
petted from above There is a swirl to our world
I feel it too swirly like an invisible currency
My work is seated now and dignified

Now when my sister takes the debit card
To the grocery store it will not be declined and now
when we put the cake on the table it will not be
stolen by a hungry child named after a luxury car
with golden hair Mercedes with your ashen face
Mayra with your lottery ball Monica and the slot
machines lining the street Sell them out for a degree
a seat at the bar a platform from which to blink
They say I must twist the key on some prison cells First
I must tie my ankle to a sector? Choke on it Fuck you Bye

My sister cut my hair to my shoulders where I could watch it

I must serve my duty to profit with this debt
An ever-present pile I take into my shovel and move from
One bed to another the rocks and red mulch expanding Beyond
the picnic tables I find a head bowed
over a poker like a staff which herds litter into a ballooning bag
while overhead the clouds are swollen with white wool
I could write a psalm for us just as soon as I'm returned
To my desk under the steeples of brick but I'm here
on the side of the highway on the bench in the courthouse
In a cell in a county jail There's flour on her forearms When

the cops burst in she was making tortillas When
the car pulled out we were high on ecstasy When
they handed back my underwear I said thank you

My father said haircuts are an art
It was the first time I'd heard him say art
I gave my split ends to my sister
My daughter a scythe

SHEPHERDS

THE CARROT AND THE STICK

A horse's exasperated approach—
two strung legs lumbering, weary-wise, with knees
like acorns in a basket, or a bank clerk's drawer, and back
legs, too, clomping toward might-as-well, might-as-well.
A girl holds out a bouquet of refrigerator rot; their eyes meet.
Every stalk she offers expired last month.
but the teeth take the wilts. Still the sway back holds.
Theirs is a courtroom tenderness—a man crying into the
scalp of the cop who killed his brother. Her apple-scented shampoo.
Sentences will be held in a rattlesnake's mouth on a desk far away.
But here, in this wiry, golden moment of hair-sensed trust,
the bouquet girl is recorded on an iPhone patting an emaciated horse.
Watching her tan shoulder, the biteable tender,
one mistakes this gesture for something better
than a carrot on a string that will twist
through grains of autoplay, slipping a bridle
around a thousand public thumbs.
A field mouse escapes the rattlesnake's mouth
and her gingham skirt brushes the gate, as if there's a message
beyond this placing on a grave a carrot with a public stick that snaps,
besides reporting animal abuse to a dog catcher
with a long pole neck, in a town of oatless people and starving horses,
where crude oil and Maw Maw's food pantry haul is off
before it gets home, spoiled as this injured land, what is happening?
Meekness is a baton traveling down a river, pausing at every dam.
Blessed are the crimes of the American poor
for they will inherit horses.

THE HEEDLESS SHEPHERD

A family is a river slipping

around every bend

It's a crime to be born poor

It's treason to stay that way

Memaw wore a red gingham apron

while plating creamed corn on the base

Back then work had a weight, you could feel it

Bearing down from mountains, a hoof

pressing us flat to seed in wide plains

Shepherd fell in love with a cherry

on the way to enlist at Fort Hood

Her daughter sat under an eye

that lost her in a blind spot

We're lethargic as mud

Angry for no reason

Our ancestors have robbed and been robbed

And now everything is a mess

WET MOON

Money is a garden
Poverty a genetic disease

I have enough
Roses for a wedding
In my bank account
And every morning
I piss blood into a well

The problem with salaries
Is they present hope

I'm looking to buy some land
In a place where I once would have
Pulled up the grass
Like soiled carpets
Just to pity the worms

Getting older is a return
On someone else's bad investment

A few thousand per acre to tend
To my ancestral maladies
Fuck it, why not?

As every poor person knows
Instincts are more reliable
Than a lucky break

Somebody's got to
Buy the farm

So the others can raise babies

And I'm rich now

My company has given me
An investment portfolio
With three managers linked in banker blue

Last week we were driving
Across the steppes of Texas
And I caught the title
"Landman" in my breath
Where it's stayed like some blunt rock

The moon doesn't flinch when it rains
As I expect it does, rain

"A known stop for sex trafficking.
Do your research."
Reads the single Wet Moon review

When refuge is toil wrapped
In the cloak of midnight
These rumors are true if not accurate

As we drive past this building
Where some people are released
And others are shackled

My retirement plan says I'll need to close
a gap of five thousand before age 35
And I think of an old currency:
Only 3.5 men

But I'm no longer my own agent
I belong to the land and it belongs to me

I belong to my money and it belongs to this tree
You belong to my dreams
Which belong to a god
Who slithers through the weeds
Of our money and its needs

I'm possessed by a landman
And that landman is me

DOWNTOWN LIQUOR

Sounds like Oz

Sounds like someone's dream of a home
Buried in chaparral set crooked on some

Dry old caliche
Where the sky burns like brush
Where your irises pale
On contact with historical talcum

El Chapo built that cool fucking tunnel
Up to the door of an empty Arizona hotel

With its smelter-bought Tiffany glass desert mural
Copper become marble; flesh become rust

For $142 a night I could be gone there,
Upstaged by a flower that blooms once a year, I could
Just book a weekend to imagine it

Last night I dreamt a baby was born
But I'd taken all the bullets out of the guns
I wasn't ready when they came

Two congressmen made it safer to kill wolves
And for 14 million people to starve

You're born a visitor and made a prisoner

Not long ago
I wasn't alone
I was carrying a village

Now the gone things
Are lodged inside me
A cluster of no-shows

It's a ghostly periphery I contain, a dead settlement,
With a disease like a pioneer's name

Because you're lucky if you can forget
Your omissions and God help you
If you make anything up, ever

Not long ago
My breasts were milky cheeks
On a body of waving wheat

I was a happy home
With so much square footage to spare

Then I was a pregnant wolf at a dog fight
Circling a ring of my own bloodlust

Sometimes I want to be worth protecting
Which would mean carrying
Someone younger towards a more distant death

My father's grandparents buried their dead
On the stomach of two hills they call
Twin Sisters

And there are twins on that side, too
And there are dead children on the other side, too

One died from dysentery when
A corpse poisoned the well

My mother's mothers' twins expired
In a shack just over those tracks

No one invented these children
We named them Fruit and Vine
They were native and never cried

It seems anything the eye touches
Can be condemned
And my Google eye can touch it all

I can finger that dust no one wants
I can shovel the roots aside

If your money breaks again
Again if it splinters into needles
For cows to chew

You can show your heart to border patrol
Let the cartels know you moved into WeWork
You're all set for today's review

As for my corporate dowry
Well, we'll see!

We're sleeping at Amazon because
I wasn't ready to shoot

I lay down a pallet for more gentle beasts
And wait for the crackling signs of commerce
To wake the next generation

I'm sorry to say we are guilty
Of having always been here

GONE TO ROSE

They drank cow's milk, ate brown eggs,
sometimes beef, bitter vegetables that
rumbled in the gut.

Since they've been gone,
we've only uprooted, practiced doom
with our chins down, looked backwards,
grumbled, slept it off.

Did they expect we'd still be broke,
acting like it's fine, farming in backyards,
never getting even.

You can stand inside a noose
and get roped in. Or you
can dodge the lasso,
but it never ends.

Here, there is nothing to steward,
but much more to do, and our roses
have granddaughters.

SHARECROPPING

They'd never been anywhere
Other than where they were.
Though the river was shallow
People will say they swam.
Though the land was supreme
They will say she was a child
In need of discipline. They'll say
She tried to strangle her nurse,
Burned her own face to shame them,
Stepped on nails and rejected medicine.
Though the prairie was an empire,
People will say it was decrepit.

They'd never been anywhere
Other than where they'd been,
And it was nothing like this.
Though they were maids,
People will say they were men.
Though they were squatters,
They had an army behind them,
And people will say they were pious,
Though they were petulant as servants
Given keys to the master's house.

There will be a legacy lottery.
Not everyone will show up to play.
The message of their protest:
Instead, they'll make the best of it.
They'll pick till their hands bled,
They'll ship off to war, grow crops
Under their skirts, bloom

A stubborn glamor of costume chiffon,
Eat pills from an Easter basket,
Grab onto an institution and ride,
Hire mariachis for the weddings,
Bagpipers for the funerals.

GUAPA Y GUAPO

She was a movie star sucking lozenges,
her hair in a pyramid, her Youth Dew
on fire as she smirked at the limes,
implacable Madonna.

He was handsome as a rifle,
brushing his suede cowboy hat,
boots cigar brown next to his bare
recliner as he unfolded his body,
a parched flag quenched with beer.

PASTORAL II

It was a spare existence
And I long for it still

Paper thin subsistence I get it
Less means less

I was a someday child of pumpjacks
Sitting atop an oil well counting my wins

Like cotton bulbs baled, there were just enough
To do it again

Once, a fake preacher made me cry
By telling me I was sad

Back then I was too pious to ask for payment

Until out of the limestone grew
A mound of fluorescent lantana

And an appetite was born

BABIES

Tell your baby
I'm their baby now

RAZE AND SHINE

There was once born a flat girl
Her mouth was opened, stuffed, and stitched.

Though the world around her is fat,
She sucks without swallowing,
She kisses like a window.

Her mother designed her that way:
As a person, only decorative.
As a brand, extremely effective.

She makes a billion dollars,
Then she puts it in a crib and turns off the lights.

MAKING UP

I had to approach her as an idea
Not yet contoured

Where she might have shrunk I picked up
Eyebrow pencils

And made her submit
Her face under my forearm

So what if my mother was more shadow
Than shade

What I see in her face, I wonder,
Does it show?

The under-eye crash diet of the soul
A mouth hiding from a voice

What if my tools dispense light

I cocked my chin to move closer
And I noticed she held her breath

The more petrified the mother
The more she fears her daughter

I would rather create something new
Out of us

But I am also being mineralized
Rapidly over ages

I have a threadbare vocabulary
A stagnant nature
Like a pond that has seen better days

So heavy in my blood
Murky and parasitic

I am making up my mother's face
In my own image,

An act not unlike forgiveness —
pruning, weeding, fondling,

Gloves on, mending wire fences

Someday I'll have a daughter
But for now, I work with what I have

Her face is diffident
Unforthcoming in a way
I'm too chicken shit to prod

My mother is a receding gale
Thunder in her own weather

The more studied a forecast
The more potent its threat

Off stage ballerinas look like cattle
After a roundup, tired, pulsing

I ran away from my mother
To wear exquisite perfume

And cradle a small dog

I've lived like a poet
And worked like a man

SURVIVANCE

The RV park she managed
Was a repository for wages.
There was nothing to do but keep tabs
And count seashells in the dirt.
Here, heads are built to resist
Intellectual poison; the schools
Put bodies back in the fields to break
Every Friday night like dirty waves
Against the offshore rigs.
Beyond the RV park is a gulf as enclosed
As a womb—incompletely.
I was taken to meet a pedophile
Whose left hand missed a thumb.
Just a stub he wiggled in my face.
In every family, there are darkened rooms
Or mothers who shut their eyes.

LUCKYSCENT

For Bridget Talone

Small absolutes vaporized into tiny uprisings, naked with promise; certain to expire. When I said God was a scent I was counting on a wiser someone's next thought. But it's true. I do believe holiness to be that which registers in spite of sight and stolid intellect. The other day I caught the sillage of a monk setting down her pen in a crevice of wet moss never to pray again. See how we exist on things that smell better than they are? When I had no money, I spent it. Now, with money, I spend it. This vulture dousing Arpege from a bottle of peacock blue is no writ of God. Poetry can't save me from being this stupid. Then again, I wonder. Smells have turned over epochs with sap and glands. Perfume can cloak you in animalic ambition. Some dry downs hang on while others hunch some trot they lion. By grace alone I smell MEM and MAAI, I huff Mitsuko, Opardu, and Melodie de L'amour. I crave cement and castor and a stone crevice plastered. Ash tilled into soil. Earwax on a stole. I want to be inhaled like a wet strip, from wet to dry. Friars palm pomegranates in the brassy morning light. The whole opera box straddles my cloud of Superstitious as we gallop up to an atomic jasmine Valhalla. I imagine our ending will have a smell we can't imagine. Waterless ambergris. Massacre of orris. God will ask, "Did you ever try to be less stupid?" I wonder.

BLACK CANAL

Outside Crazy Horse... in Paris, France!
I clasp a CEO in one hand,
A glass of Sancerre in the other.

Papé used to say, "I'm going to get drunk
And be someone."

My dress is a milkmaid gingham,
Exuding sensual peasantry.
I'm a prized experience from anywhere,
Bright as the Lucite appendage
Attached to a dancer's knee, a prism
Under stage lights, a swamp nymph
Who escaped to an apartment
With turquoise walls and kittens
The size of tennis balls.

Pleasure is an identity requiring consumption.
I placed two orange shopping bags
From Le Bon Marché on Emile Zola's grave.

I've never been inside the bar where he drank,
But I've heard shoes aren't required.
I've met his extramarital lover, I witnessed
The hours before his death
When visions of dead loved ones came to him,
Proving he'd been someone.

PARIS MY DAUGHTER

Aus einem April
and blue globes skitter the rails of my heart
I weep, of course

It's November
A vegetal rot rises stripping
the bowels of dipping pools
at the Diplomat Resort & Spa in Hollywood, Florida
where I am besotted

to be expository—

Deacons of plume States
Elders of scrim
Mene Mene Tekel Upharsin
Time for a King James hymn

My father avoided me for years
and to this day I can't stand
a short-breathed drunk
in an old slaver's forest

which has the syllabic quality of folk wisdom
but means literally nothing

and moves less than
a pulse

Lately there's a great need for prose
for rows of drowning does

No, ugh, I'm
sorry I'm not sorry

When verses scan the sand like sulfur
the air is limp
It fans infections toward farmers
who pipe slowly
the only words they have:
I remember

Antiseptic are they in the wounds of the long occupied
tight in the cartilage of soldiers

Really though, poetry requires concession
The inexpressible falls out in clots
getting expressed nonetheless in the process

Narrative, on the other hand, is like an antibiotic
that peels out disease
along with everything good

I'm not blaming medicine or prose
for what demagogues are saying these days
but I do take my short lines in earnest to the interstices
and make them to lie down across the shifting public needle
like a campaign of form

I'm sorry I allow despair to enter every day
I'm sorry for denying my frailties

There's a land of bays where I trade heat for deliverance
I'm sorry for that, too

Prose is a peacetime genre
for the predictably defeated—

Literary Naturalism?
Secure in its echoes, reverberations, and repeatability...

All my fathers have pink faces
that sucker at me like Texas Rangers
When Christendom lives in the era of posts
it hoists a daughter upon you and says
Shoot me your vote

If she remains
If she remains

What an overworked father gleans from a Shah's generosity
has worried me since I was young

So when someone says you cannot write heart like that
in the second line of a poem
I tell them

Heroic Hall of Fame athlete biopics failed
to kick through my walls
When I sagged into a new form of myself
 the social balance eventually leavened

For this I owe my weak mindedness
and trotting superficial charms

In this edification I ask for plain tenderness
I regard my father's psychic knots

squeeze his hand
and sprint away

Today I am not ashamed of my primitive bray for note
or what I copy and paste from Social Realism
to slake my coarse cravings
for local upheaval

When I write "I" it's to draw a crowd around me

Recall the spilled blood of silk horses
O Cyrus, my sad-sweet jock
King of Kings of a media dominion

He says he likes gangster shit
I like it too
Spill your childhood trauma in my war purse
and your seed in my shower

Every April my father and I both try to surrender

Conquer my life, say "I want to
make love to you" in Persian
Think only of what will separate me from all but you
Give me a daughter to guard
Give me your daughterless mother
Chain me to a gestalt safe from polytheism
Make me
serve the gulf like a priestess

White birds drift over tilled black fields
They nestle in like cotton burs

It's January
Waves from November recede in my heart
The words, "I've met someone,"
are the fourth star
on a Yelp review
timid at the wheel of a great accrued boredom

I weep of course
I have a brother but he died he says
Me too I have a brother who died
but he is not yet dead

We were too 6th century BC
The ocean threw us out into a retiree's cabana
and made me ask you about shootings in Paris

Paris, you said,
is the daughter of the world

When she is defiled, fathers
are wild to stab

When the daughter is glorious
they tend their promising grapes

When she is a whore
they make New Age excuses
provided by women attending work conferences

Rain trebles a classic rock song in Queens
The theme is multi-generational returns

Children are begging at the gates
Cities after fall are imminent

I can admit
that in our lifetimes we may be killed
by opposing extremist groups
perhaps while facing each other
and that scares me
and makes me more in love with you

Worst of all, as we make deals inside of history,
we're oblivious
to the chokedness of it all

We know not how to leave our cities
We know not how to forget an empire
Because of thin prosperity we can lock gazes
over martinis, silver toothpicks spearing olives

Fawnish marble and cherries, we wonder,
We kiss, or do we, my victory? Do we, my stranger?

Your dead brother who was
an artist like me I was one
I am I was
one too—
as well
Because you have no respect for origins

And why should you given the circumstances
And yet it's a belief in home that makes
most violence possible

And I think because you said you like America
because it's fun
you are capable of
I don't know what

Loose body glitter blows across a family line
and I suffer less when the person I'm seducing
gets nervous

And soon very soon I know the stomach of civilization
will rupture
and reveal where we've been treading water

among rose-infused ice cubes
that will float us higher
into the blades of a divine umbrella

And part of this undoing will still be fun
like America is fun

My patriarchs reach me through bagpipes
saying they wish I could be sorry enough

As pressure drops in the air like hooves
I get out of the car and text:

It's April

MUSK

Months, sometimes years,
Go by with no results.
But I don't forget to wear perfume.
Peasants and saints are in fashion
And rising yeast is a fad.
If you throw your crust on a stone
A bird probably won't come.
Mid-gestation I'm a stick in the mud
And a volcano stirring the ocean
Blending salt with molecules and algae
In a creation that's beginning again.
This time heavier and woolen
Like a Victorian bathing suit pooling
Around a woman's midsection
While a lake does what it does: lies there.
I almost can't stand the smell
Of my own body with its hidden fluids
Which keep me safe and animal
Bound up in survival
When I want to live, just really live!

SPLEEN

It's a cool summer indolent and blank
Why must I write to write?
With machines created in my likeness
I lunge at tremors of thought
I throw dead weight behind my knuckles
And still, no one needs this

Nothing is more tyrannical than time
Which saves the crumpled receipt
My poor planning has caused a person
To deliver food in unfriendly weather
I'm depressed, but it will pass
Quickly like summer

RISING FURIES

In an hour I'll be researching luxury consumer searches, which
Puzzles me because I thought the whole point of being
A luxury consumer was that you didn't search. Instead
You are a member of various tiered groups, you are
At the top of a customer pyramid, it is
A strategy for building customer loyalty and CLV, that is
Customer Lifetime Value, but now
I guess the luxury consumer market is changing, like it
Wasn't immersive enough for spenders to absorb pleasure
Packaged in an emblazoned red aura of rewards. To be
Rich is to spend less money on products,
Get more experiential perks, says data.
They want everyone else's experience too. They want
The search engine gratification, they like
The hunt and to be delighted and surprised. Who doesn't
Want to feel horseradish vodka sizzling over an ice luge? I'm so
Inundated with lilac promises of fame—just kidding.
But lately I've wondered if I'll soon get money. When you
Get money, says the poem, When I
Get money? I respond strongly to diction. You can't
Always get what you want, my parents
Would sing to us when we asked for things, with
A mean, glinting glee. Joy is
Sharing domination and the art of everyday terror
With a spouse with whom you've made
Irreversible mistakes that still feel trivial but someday,
This day, will become a whole life of wrongheaded impulse buys.
My last few weeks with Eve Babitz in *Slow Days, Fast Company*
Took me back to the desert where my discontent
Became tangible, a lemon floating topside in tonic. I was
Starting fights I couldn't finish. In the

Hot tub I said I wanted things I don't, I watched
The shadow where I knew a mountain stood. I am
Too old to date famous men or cash in on charisma, I can,
However, work spinningly and pleasantly, at a distance.
It is a kind of leisure to watch the figures you once knew
Become hallucinations in the long waves of a spent day.

SEE MORE LIKE THIS

I am simple and virtuous
But my country moneys my layette
She lays my banquette on the line.
Baby is on my breast as I cane the hills
Red rivers stain my ankles.

I confess to collaborating with those I hate
And forgetting to tend my flock.

In the herd your values won't excel.
They calculate us, they target us
Inside milk white sheets of cells.

They browse the edges of territories
To see performance by region.

Employment is a strange country
Its loves are not my loves.

I am simple and virtuous.
While my baby sleeps, I shop.

GUNS

ANTHEM

The graduates are bought.

Let us put them somewhere in consulting.

Liberty lived a decent life

Which no one can remember.

As we pursued happiness

Our own thumbprints bit our heels.

We became unfamiliar with prudence.

Our most obvious manners looked heroic.

We marched and didn't progress.

Our limits became commendable.

Only the ones exempt from precarity

Made names in service.

Speaking in a compassionate tone

They kept it all intact.

Let us send a herd to trample the market.

She's devoured my hours.

She's shrunk my life.

We'll be a nation of repossessed time

A public vengeance with no army.

All that was going is already gone.

THE QUESTION OF EVIL

I have my bones, dim leisure, hard sense.
When my daughter comes, she will live
Where people who are better than me
Had their babies wrenched from their arms,
Scattered to the winds.

At best, I can do an interpretation of justice
And hope it doesn't go up in smoke.
I'm a human enlisted by organizations
In the act of humanizing, and I'm a person
moving through a world, as they say.
I can believe what I do is valuable,
Or I can just wait and see.

I can be like a gallon of water
Hidden behind the bald rock, like a can
Of beans feeding children in the desert.
When I sleep I'm just a rock,
Layers of minerals and data,
And my dreams speak for everyone.

BAKED ALASKA BOMBES

I can't see you
But I know you to be somewhere.
Heaux la bombes icing
Across the night.
In our dumb, we flutter at you.
Cold star encased with pastry.
Toasted sequins rain on the desert,
They fall as crust to sand white
Ashlettes melted on rubble, cotton,
Kitten tongues, we cannot scream.
Sleep is a dream that got dizzy
Circling a silent foaming fountain.
Right outside our windows
Night rips open her dress
Revealing silver jackhammers
Stuttering out sharp tinsels of pain.
Every hour unfolds a rapture,
Brushing cheeks with tentacles,
Wrapping hills in phantom warfare,
Ordering lightning before thunder, blue eels
Swerve in a tundra where even sobriety dries out.
Your hiddenness bombes slice me,
You're a long arc knifed between what I know
And what I suspect is always happening.

HUSH

We are marching to Ciudad Juarez in my heart
To execute you against the fence
I told my colleagues I was leaving my post
And they congratulated me in secret
How grotesquely your overslept lips droop
When you pretend you've suffered
Over time these mouths grow longer thinner
My uncle is a corrupt DEA agent
Like a coup
He thinks in terms of denial and glory
When I remove this maternity dress
You'll see a thousand muscles galvanized
By the singular taste of overthrow
It is all I can do to stay in the tender zone
And it's not going to be enough
To feed this peculiar taste which
Prefers being betrayed to betrayal

SAN MARCOS

Since I stopped the flow
Of impressionable men
Whom I'd thoughtlessly collect,
And from whom the spring feeds,
Without explanation, I have been
Shopping so much more
Than suits a prophet in the forest.

One said he felt ashamed,
But an admission as such
Does not irrigate a dry spell
Once it's surpassed the length
Of a petty offense record.

A body's memory is not so
Distorted by language
And there's little enjoyment in force
When the subject is inertia.

I used to leave as soon as
The molecules stabilized, but
Now I am both the one who stays
And the one who leaves.

Novelty is difficult and common
And each design reforms
The future and the first.

MY THIRST

You see the reason I had
To deliver you to the bank
Where the clangor of my causes
Could not rouse your fiscal ugliness
Was externally determined
As only aridity can produce
Terranean worship of my body as a passage.

There was no chill within me
At least not any undamaged by age.

I had to go again in pursuit
Of shaved diamonds
And pill queens wearing jumpsuits.
I had to devote myself to cashmere chew toys
And create calendar reminders of self-regard.

But you are your own pet coward now
Led like a gelding by a satin ribbon.
And I may be less deceived
But I'm also less adored.

Beware of too-verdant land, I say
Beware of cultivated men.
Now we dig a trench
And your women ask us why
And, you dolt, you have no answer.

The future will depend on iteration
And the key cards of entrepreneurs
Who are self-professed business hippies.

Soon every person will have been let down
By a man who buys antiques online.

SERMON

You see there are rich people
And there are poor people
And then there are cops

Rich people
helping poor people
become acceptably poor
Between them: cops

Some poor people
Become rich people
And find several uses for cops

Some poor people become cops
And receive invitations from rich people

There are three types of people:
Rich people, poor people, cops
And between them—philanthropy

Greed eats the pit and all
And charity provides coating

At the end of the gala
we ask for the centerpieces
Going home with full vases
The chrysanthemums
Gorgeous to eat

PROPHYLACTICS

Pesticides	Pregnancy	Stress	Automated
Savings	Weapons	Seasons	
Monuments	Credit	Insurance	Excess
Narcissism	Wellness Checks	Retail	Algorithms
Probation	Overtime	Privacy Gain	
Highways	Clout	Cremation	Sanitation
Debt	Passwords	Shapewear	Sports
Fear	Mortgages	Museums	Beauty
Self-Care	Timesheets	Convenience	Reputation

Payments   Suburbs   Likes

Donations   Nations   Wages   Fines

Retirement Plans Caution

Central Heat & Air

Personal Style   Live Feeds

Streaming   Bladders   Celebrity

SUVs   Doormen   Vanity

Bonuses   Awards

Prisons   Foundations

I DON'T BELIEVE IN PRESIDENTS

For Ana Božičević

The President is a rose, She is
The woman of the world.
From her thorns the nation is armed,
And the wail of the Midnight Special
Is an earthquake to a flower.
Night bloomers, we raise you,
We cosset your dark acts.
Any way it goes, someone will have to
Pretend to cum.

IT'S QUIET BUT IT'S NOT STILL

It's difficult to know
What kind of pain is unacceptable
Mostly, I am tempered,
Enfolded in my intellect, which is sufficient
And stylish, but not great.
Often, a damp rodent sits on my chest
And my waves are nervous whiskers.
Sometimes, not a single feeling strikes me,
And I wish there was an emergency to fix.
But always the father is almost home.
When he gets here, he'll be displeased.
I made my man's home look crazy.
When I look at it, I see prairies
From books, wheat fields flirting
With a cornflower blue sky.
It's my fault, this discontent,
That awkward corner where the lamp
Fails to hide a jumble of chords.

SERVING MANY MASTERS

Products are easy.
People can be solved.
I picked up the dinner tab
And managed some previously
Unthinkable forms of diplomacy.
I buttoned up my shirt at an auction,
Stood well-heeled
On the bottom line.
Robin Hood spoke at the ball
To agents of change in righteous thrall.
I was demure inside evil-as-usual,
Perfecting a work/work balance.
I reserved a private hospital room,
Pinched my nose.
Nothing shocks me
When I'm serving many masters—
Nothing, not even the clap in the crawl,
Or immigration law, or when
We ask why we do this,
And they answer not at all.
Here's the one you call
Paw Paw come to take you
On back to the farm.
Don't get up if you're not
Ready to crawl.

REVENGE

I brush it from my forehead
I spill it on my wrists
I pull it up in an incognito window
I smother it with soap beads
I smear it across my thigh
I watch it snail in the sunlight
It drains from a root
I wake up and take pills for it
I warned them about it
When it billowed over steeples
I took it to the treatment plant
I wiped it on closed tanks
I changed its name in LastPass
But I remembered it anyway
It expected quarterly results
It restarted with a chime
So I hummed it back to sleep

PASTORAL III

Someday child wants to sleep forever
On the job I lie down in green pastures

Now there are acres on which to become
Precious, kept, and lovely

I was given a rod so fine
So full of wrath, a lamb so plump
With a lion's share

Wolves carried my message on their fangs
To cities where gates jingle
And slaughterhouses overflow

Money, they say, is uninhabitable

But I promise
My sheep will guard you as I have guarded them

And in this way, you'll never owe

THE GONE THING

We tried to go home with ourselves

But when we got there our labor stood

Magnificently tall in a blue robe of light flickering

She's a long glassy tooth that we kiss

Goodnight tomorrow I will fill up my cart

And push it with one hand and with the other

I will press loose units to my breast

I have come to the hot room to work

Washing paint from a screen and clicking boards

Not every person has worked do you know

If you've worked about the chicken fryer

Or been sentenced to work in debt to those

Entities which don't work but operate

Which have given us debt

Everything flows from those who do nothing

For free in the cold room I had come

To work in steadfast devotion to a capability

Which would give me a voice in high places

Something to look at under tables sat

With owners who will unlearn my daughter of work

In the restaurants and the strip clubs

And fields of unprofessional care

All riches flow from ideas that don't work at home

Because we have nothing to give we give them our give

We are serving intellectual minnows who take

Our most common deeds and build from them concepts

We yielded our daydreams we branded

Grandma's handwritten poem her unrecorded beauty

And the secret of cotton dead from too much watering

Most of the time we are ducks caught in rapids

We have chosen it over the still pond

Across the meadow We are admired for

Our sputtering sacrifice when the clouds part

A voice says you deserve this

And we bob to accept the white water in our bills

Everything we have flows from those financials

Which illuminate nothing

All day I gestate another era of co-signs

I gather no crops in my palms I tend instead to hours

Those trees in the valley have learned to curtsy low

To the wind Now where did they get this idea?

Blue fucking pastoral says the boss in my case

When the lawyer comes to spill your song

Just try to go home with yourself They'll pry

Open your tweets The boss has no money Nice try

I have to work with the banners A dirge with gloss

And the sales within them tremble with bonus

We tried to earn enough to go home

But the quarter was weak

Go down great losers of history for we are

Human resources so precious so vast are we

That they must bury us in the ground to extract

You later like the heroes you are fined to be

You see money's in the valley and glory's in the fees

When the boss speaks no one is the boss

We must follow the work as it matures into rest

Remember to take the pill that makes you ill

Enough to perform at the top You're an earner

As well as a mother You're a midwife to conversions

When you go home with yourself you enter

A new market You tap against your own glass You

Lie down in the shape of a kidney and stare

Who are you dithering in the open Not

Trying to be rich or remembered Don't you

Know there are those who gave us all one price

We walked up through miles of iron hills past

Broken egg towns with the doors ajar revealing

Today's Walmart deals and entrepreneurs sitting

With their legs cut off below the knees They wave

A bruised plaque an upturned tin We grow old

In a series of twitches drinking beer on the slab of a garage

One road led to the train trellis where the river

And the blind blood of teenagers made it sweet enough

For a while to have never seen a Grecian urn behind

Layers of metaphor or marked a marble stair

With my heel I have tried to walk above myself

Only to end up romanticizing

The wrong side of the tracks

The money long as a clean flight home

I once saw the prom king stabbed on a mossy rock

His blood washed in the current What could be more

Tragic than never having the chance to pick a career

Path or stock portfolio to run a check into a slot

With a glowing blue mouth that accepts it

On the island of Naoshima the James Turrell made

A woman cry out, "Help me! I can't see" and simply it was death

We all felt it which is common and profound Easy

To reckon with but so much duller to face without light

I've decided to die eyes open after seeing some things that

Make me want to live forever

Like the faces pinched between gasping

Waterlilies issued from a man's pastel despair

And if you'd never been with a redhead in Paris or

Lost by the Tiber or tongue kissed in Lisbon or at the bottom

Of a limestone quarry or facing the long scream of beauty

Of course it would seem the hometown river runs endlessly

Forever low except when it's too high and it's possible

To drown by only a fingertip having seen no Lucite stairs

Leading up to a temple of solvency and promissory

What we're saying is I'm going to kick over the ladder

Once I get to the top and you're going to knock

Your kids back a few rungs and she's going to decline

This metaphor altogether in favor of keeping growth

In check while acknowledging her great privilege to do so

Others can be paid to hold the base of the ladder

By giving up a turn to ascend it

We trade merits for knicks inside grains of wood

We stifle our wants with soggy petals

Firmly my debts have taken me in the night on wild

Parachute glides They come as sprites to my bed

Carrying me across the economic landscape

Pointing out the private sector in seductive terms Embracing me

Like a lender who can bury you or marry you

But instead holds your breath in her mouth forever

Back to what I was saying We're going to build our own

And if that doesn't work we will take someone else's

At the stake they'll burn all the ladders up to Valhalla

Someday upon my honor mercy will prevail for the unladdered

Says the laddered as she curls the rung in her arch

We tried to go home but the way was lost

I am trying to make our home in a baby

Won't we try to yield fruit once again I am

What I am so I repeat this prayer that we will

All go back to earth before we are returned there wrongly

Fallen off ladders like spun weathervanes after taxes

Poor machinery pointing the children nowhere

We tried to take nothing home with us except for

The many ropes we thought to re-braid

From when we tied our gait from here to there

Expecting an eventual croon Take nothing home
Except your defiant laziness your angry exhaustion
Tomorrow I will pull a new hum
While holding a payment in my throat

This would be a hymn
It would be stiff lingerie opened in an SUV
It would be a collection on unpaid overtime
It would buy plastic wrapped shirts at the mall
And soothe the stubs of unlovable feelings
We have pressed inside us a handful of truths
Such as time is an accumulation of tense surrenders
You resisted but couldn't prevent
And the sex of money is a blue icicle too hard to melt
She shakes her head "no" while mouthing "yes"

I tried to perform work instead of working and it worked
Much better under the newest circumstances
And with this diploma I ate and drank and paid for it
With the parts of my body that meant nothing to me
This problem you will come to recognize as another's

Arrived with me and will go with you too

Because we can't let it sink

can't afford it

ACKNOWLEDGMENTS

First, thank you to Jake for being my home, and for sheltering me in the mountains where I could be barefoot and pregnant and free for a while. Thank you to Lantana for keeping me company as I wrote most of these poems to the rhythm of your in-utero dancing. Thank you to the earliest readers and champions of this manuscript, Karl Johnson and Mira Goral. Thank you to Kim Rosenfield for leading me to Matvei Yankelevich. Thank you to Matvei for being who you are and doing what you do. I'm grateful to be among the admirable writers who have benefitted from your imagination and diligence. Thank you to Madeleine Maillet, John Goldbach, Caroline Gormley, Logan Fry, Coco Fitterman, Rebekah Alaniz, Aaron Alaniz, Emily Brandt, Ben Fama, Elaine Kahn, Olivia Orley, Laura Marie Marciano, Brenda Shaughnessy, Craig Teicher, Laura Henriksen, Shiv Kotecha, Rainer Diana Hamilton, Dorothy Chan, Kim Calder, Brandon Brown, Forsyth Harmon, and Peter BD for encouraging me.

Thank you to the editors of *Blush Lit*, *Flag + Void*, *The Recluse*, *Leavings Lit*, *Poetry Society of America*, *Poetry Foundation*, *Salt Hill*, and *Wonder* for publishing poems from this book.

MONICA MCCLURE is a Brooklyn-based writer and author of the poetry collection, *Tender Data* (Birds, LLC, 2015) and the chapbooks *Concomitance* (Counterpath Press, 2016), *Boss Parts 1&2* (If A Leaf Falls Press, 2016), *Mala* (Poor Claudia, 2014), and *Mood Swing* (Snacks Press 2013). With Madeleine Maillet and Emily Brandt, she runs Yellow Wallpaper, an organization that promotes radically and rigorously curated books and book culture for readers outside major metropolitan areas. She works as a copywriter for e-commerce and tech.